Antony McDeere

WHITTLING
FOR BEGINNERS
AND KIDS

"Quick & Easy Whittling projects illustrated step by step, to carve from wood unique objects for your original gifts"

Table of contents

INTRODUCTION

Wood carving is a form of woodworking by means of a cutting tool (knife) in one hand or a chisel in two hands or with one hand on a chisel and one hand on a mallet, resulting in a wooden figure or a figurine, or in a sculptural ornamentation of a wooden object. The term may also refer to the finished product, from individual pieces to hand-crafted moldings that make up part of the tracery.

Wood sculpture has been highly commonly made, but it lasts even less well than other large materials such as stone and bronze, as it is vulnerable to rot, insect damage and burning. It is therefore an important secret item in the art history of many cultures. Outdoor wood sculptures do not last long in most parts of the world, so it is still unclear how the totem pole tradition has grown. Many of the most important sculptures in China and Japan, in general, are made of wood, and so are the vast majority of African sculptures and those in Oceania and other continents. Wood is light and can accommodate very fine detail so that it is particularly appropriate for masks and other objects to be used and mounted. It is also much easier to work on than stone. Some of the finest examples of early European wood carvings are from the Middle Ages in Germany, Russia, Italy and France, where the typical themes of that era were Christian iconography. Throughout England, some complete examples exist from the 16th and 17th centuries, where oak was the preferred medium.

A carver of wood begins a new carving by selecting a piece of wood of the approximate size and shape of the figure that he or she wants to make or, if the carving is to be large, several pieces of wood may be laminated together to create the required size. The quality of wood is very significant. Hardwoods are more difficult to mold, but they have a greater luster and durability. Softer woods may be easier to cut, but they are more prone to damage. Every wood can be carved, but all of them have different qualities and characteristics. The choice would depend on the criteria of carving: for example, a precise figure would need a fine-grained wood and a very small figure, as a large figure might conflict with the' reading' of fine detail.

Once the sculptor has selected their wood, he or she starts a general cycle of carving using gouges of different sizes. The gouge is a smooth knife that can softly cut large portions of the wood. In the case of hard woods, the sculptor may use sharpened gouges with stronger bevels, around 35 degrees, and a mallet similar to a stone carver. Terms like gouge and chisel is subject to misunderstanding. Correctly, a gouge is a curved cross-section device, and a chisel is a straight cross-section tool. Nevertheless, skilled carvers tend to refer to all of them as' chisels.' Smaller sculptures may require the woodcarver to use a knife, and larger pieces may require the use of a saw. No matter what kind of wood is used and what kind of tool is used, the wood sculptor must always carve whether through or with the grain of the wood, never against the grain.

Once a basic shape has been made, the carver may use a variety of tools to build images. Of example, a "veiner" or "fluter" can be used to make deep gouges on the surface or a "v-tool" to make fine lines or decorative cuts. Once the finer details have been applied, the surface of the woodcarver is finished. The method chosen depends on the quality of the surface finish required. The hardness left by deep gouges brings' strength' to the surface of the carving, and many carvers enjoy this' tooled' finish.

General smoothing can be achieved with devices such as "rasps," which are flat-bladed tools with a surface of pointed teeth, if a completely smooth surface is needed. "Rifflers" are similar to rasps, but shorter, usually double-ended, and of different shapes for operating in folds or crevasses. The fine polishing is achieved with abrasive material. Large grained paper with a rougher surface is used first, with the sculptor then with fine grained paper that can make the surface of the sculpture smooth to the touch. After carving and finishing, the artist can seal and paint the wood with a variety of natural oils, such as walnut or linseed oil, which protects the wood from dirt and humidity. Oil also imparts a shine to the wood, which, by reflecting the sun, allows the viewer to' sense' the form. Carvers often use gloss lacquer as it produces a layer that is too reflective, reflecting so much light that it can distort the shape; carvers refer to it as' toffee apple influence.' Objects made of wood are often coated with a coat of wax that covers the wood and provides a light lustrous shine. The wax finish (e.g. shoe polish) is relatively fragile but only suitable for indoor carvings.

History

Wood whittling started when people learned how to mold a piece of wood into different forms, making it one of the first methods for artistic expression. Whittling, however, did not become a common sport in the United States until the Civil War of 1865, when soldiers with skilled hands and spare hours strove to pass the time. Whittling became a popular pastime that involved men, commanding officers, and even General Ulysses S. Grant. Some soldiers who had the habit of carrying folding jack knives had become skilled whittlers. They made wood into walking sticks, figurines, dolls, smoking pipes, torches, whistles, and a cage bat. After the war, the same men taught the soldiers, enlisted in the Indian and Spanish-American wars, how to whit.

Several veterans of the Civil War were seasonal and itinerant workers who worked on railroads, ranches, plantations, and construction sites. Wherever they found work, migrant farm workers, also known as' Hoe boys,' or' Hobos,' carried their hoes with them to cultivate crops. Some traded products made from whittling in exchange for food, clothes, and shelter.

Wood whittlers are speculating that a hobo has trained Ernest "Mooney" Warther, a popular whittler, to whittle a pair of pins. The Smithsonian Institution considered Warther's sculptures to be' priceless works of art.' Whittling carried on from the Great Depression, which allowed boys to keep making things with their pocket knives. The G.I. during World War

II. Bill allowed veterans to receive college education to gain employment in industries such as manufacturing and construction. As a result, whittling began to lose ground as an important talent. The Boy Scouts, however, introduced whittling as one of the skills leaders needed to learn in the 1950s. The Boy Scouts also funded a whittling competition.

Whittling came out in 1965 with the advent of the electronic age when consumers shifted their attention to entertainment instead of hands-on activities. Public schools also discontinued their industrial and hands-on classes, limiting exposure to students who may have been interested in these skills.

Woodcarving grew slightly in the mid-1970s, with woodcarving clubs appearing here and there across the nation. Many of these membership organizations have sponsored woodcarving seminars that have taught basics. Woodcarving enthusiasts continue to strive for an upsurge in whittling interest, but have so far yielded minimal results from younger generations.

How to Whittle Whittlers need a wooden block and a pocket knife to get started. Until playing with hardwoods, experts recommend softwoods to beginners. Choose a straight grain wood to avoid carving in different directions. Do not use wood with grain defects like big knots. Basswood, pine and balsa are the most common wood used for whittling. Choose a pocket knife for the first time projects. Special knives for experienced whittlers are available for purchase; and it is recommended that these knives be sharpened with stone and strop before starting a project.

Approach whittling with caution, wear gloves or use a thumb pad to protect yourself from cuts and gauze. Whittlers who rush through a project have a better chance of injury than those who take their time.

Take a look at the wood and find the direction of the grain to determine its usability. Whittlers can make small, shallow cuts in their wood if the direction of the grain can not be deciphered. Whittlers who cut the grain will notice that the wood peels away smoothly. Conversely, cuts made against the grain are harder to peel without splitting the wood.

Whittlers have the option to choose between different cuts. For example, the straight rough cut consists of making long, sweeping cuts with the grain. Evitate cutting too deep to save the wood from splitting. The cut of the pull stroke resembles the act of paring the apple. Whittlers hold the wood in their left hand while holding the wood with their right thumb. Next, they make short, controlled strokes while keeping their thumbs away from the knife blade. The push stroke cutting technique requires both thumbs placed on the back of the blade, followed by pushing the blade forward through the wood. The push-and-pull stroke gives the whittler greater control over the knife.

WHAT IS WHITTLING

Whittling is an addictive hobby experienced by millions of individuals around the globe. It's very easy to do, and you don't need complicated or costly instruments to get began. If you're searching for data about whittling, you've come to the correct location. Here, beginners are most welcome! Even if you don't know where to begin, our supreme whittling manual will demonstrate you how to whit like a specialist. Let's get began now!

Whittling isn't a fresh hobby. It has been around since guy first created sharpening instruments thousands of years earlier. Whittling is simply shaving a piece of wood with a carving knife for a specific layout. It could be a face, a form, or anything in between. When it goes to whittling, there is no overall standard. All you need is a bit of softwood and a high-quality blade knife produced of tempered steel for the highest consequence. A sharpening stone for whittling is also suggested.

Whittling is a lot distinct from wood carving, because it's simpler and needs almost no ability at all. It also has a rougher texture, which makes it sound very handmade. Any newbie could begin whittling in a matter of minutes. Of course, there are some rules and methods that you need to familiarize yourself with in order to get the most out of your whittling project thoughts.

WHAT BEGINNERS SHOULD KNOW ABOUT WOOD WHITTLING

There are some significant variables to consider before beginning to whittle. This will render your whittling project thoughts simpler to achieve and more pleasant.

Wood Types: It is suggested that only soft wood be used when whittling. They are more malleable and can be readily sculpted with little attempt. Soft wood, like butternut and basswood, is a pleasure to whit. Hardwood, such as white oak and even mahogany, should be prevented if you value your side.

Knife: In addition, the knife used is also very essential. The finest whittling knife is provided by a strong hardened steel blade with a big and convenient handle. The handle is generally produced of resin and has an ergonomic structure that fits well in the hand. This helps to reduce hand fatigue and lets you whit for longer stretches of moment.

Project Type: If you are a beginner, begin with an simple project. Most beginners ' whittling books have easy projects that will get you began straight away.

Resources to Learn About Whittling: Books are not the only way to know how to whit. There are also a lot of helpful assets you can discover internet. Later in this manual, we will list some extra resources for your enjoyment reading.

BEST WOOD FOR WHITTLING

As mentioned above, softwood is the finest wood for beginners to whittling. They're a lot simpler to operate with. Once you've acquired some abilities, you can migrate on to easier and better wood like Mahogany. The end is worth it. Hardwood also takes much longer than soft wood and tends to have a stronger form and texture over moment.

In addition, we suggest that you use wood with straight grains. Even if the wood is a bit rough, like butternut, it's not really a issue as soon as the grains of the wood are directly. They're easier to cut and don't "chip" the wood in the wrong direction.

But there's still one issue. There are hundreds of softwoods that can render the decision a bit awkward. To assist you, here are some of the finest trees in the forest. They can readily be discovered in any lumber yard.

Basswood: a dark gray softwood with a very good grain. It's highly simple to break through and perfect for beginners. You can use basswood with a pocket knife, but a specialist whittling knife gives you a stronger outcome. Because it's so smooth, basswood is one of the finest wood for beginners.

Balsa: It's another softwood that appears comparable to basswood, except that it's a little darker brown. The grains are straight, and it's just as simple to whit. Balsa appears to turn yellow-brown as you whit. This is a prevalent feature of this wood, and there's nothing to care about.

Butternut: It's one of the most common whittling wood out there. It's got larger and larger grains, but it's just as simple to operate with as it chips away very quickly. It's also a common wood that can be discovered in most of the lumber yards. With a bit of luck, you can even get it for free.

Twigs and Branches: Who would have guessed that? One of the strengths of whittling is that you can operate with branches and roots. That's correct, man! Unlike what you might believe, stems and leaves are great materials to operate with because they are highly malleable and smooth. You can create decorations or ornamental items with them, and best of all, they're totally free of charge! Fallen trees and branches are going to operate just fine for your whittling activities.

Finding Green Wood For Carving

I believe there's a lot to say about the identification and acquisition of excellent wood for carving.

How do you begin the method of transforming a living tree into something like a Windsor chair? Which tree, exactly? This is my first issue. It's an elementary issue, and usually it's the first stage in creating something out of green wood.

When I observe or assist Kenneth fall down a tree and witness that part of the forest becomes a spoon or a chair (or, more lately, a ladder to our son's space) I discover it a enormous and magical metamorphosis.

From raw materials to items that most individuals would need to get out of their credit cards.

Kenneth has a profound and natural understanding of woodcraft from many years of working with wood, spending a lot of moment in the forest, and being a wood hoarder.

He usually leaps straight into what wooden stuff he's supposed to do and how to create them. His selection of wood and how to get it, from my point of view, appears very fluid and simple, he's usually got wood in his hands, all the time.

But as I said, I realize that this essential phase of the method needs to be detailed: where is green wood to be found? And what kind of wood is perfect for you?

This time in the method of job on green wood is a very immediate link to the forest. It is an empowering and enlightening effort to be prepared to distinguish trees and shrubs, and then to use that understanding to make helpful and lovely things.

I believe it talks to our hunter-gatherer, foragers and helps create the earth a friendlier place, just as owning a garden can link us to nature and assist us feel safer and more skilled.

So I questioned Kenneth to offer some details and history on how, where and what he decides for green wood carving.

Since he was born and raised in Atlanta, he has had some good advice, particularly for urban carvers.

WHERE TO LOOK FOR WOODS

"I've found that there's generally more wood around here in Maine than I have time to carve. I'm particularly interested in hunting wood that's already down and attached to a wood stove or to be dismissed. I'm always surprised how much wood is available if you understand where it's possible that you'd never have to bring anything out of a living tree and still have a little bit of wood to c.

Some Specific Species To Look For

As a particular rule, if a tree or shrub generates fruit or nuts, even non-edible ones, it will usually be a great option for carving.

The wood should have a uniform density and a narrow, relatively stable layer and a strong pit (the middle point of the stem or limb).

I grew up and spent most of my moment on the south shore of the United States, so excuse those who reside in separate areas, it is feasible that the types I mention do not develop wherever you are.

However, the overall law on fruit or nuts refers to any region.

Some of the excellent species here in Maine are lilac, apple, beech and hornbeam. These four are some of the tougher, more sophisticated trees for carving around here. To get started, or if you feel like your fingers need a break, attempt a white birch or a red maple.

Rhododendron and mountain laurels are okay for painting in Southern Appalachia. In fact, "Spoon Wood" is a regional name for Mountain Laurel.

The black birch, the tulip, the cherry, the walnut, and the American tree are all nice. The Southern or Frasier family of magnolias are excellent options. Any fruit tree, such as cherry, apple, plum, plum, dogwood or mulberry, is a good choice.

The perfect carving woods are those with a coherent density and near grain, rather than open or ring-shaped porous grain.

Such continuously thick woods will allow you to carve more detail and attain crisp facets and shiny tool marks.

Wood that is more porous, with separate densities between early and late increasing rings, can be difficult to carve, because your knife moves a lot between soft and hard rings as you push your knife along. It's going to be tough, consistent cuts.

If you carve a spoon of some kind of very porous wood, those pores might wind up on some of your edges. If this is the situation, the fabrics will be brittle and hard, they will appear to have a harsh texture.

The surface of your sculpture will appear rough, and there will be no description of your readings. It's also going to be difficult to get a clean surface when you're oiling and finishing your project.

Southern Yellow Pine is an example of wood with an inconsistent grain density between early growth rings and late growth rings. Examples of forests with a more consistent density are Bass wood or White Birch.

Once you discover wood, here are a few items to notice and consider green timber: we're mostly talking about using what's called green wood versus dry wood.

It's okay to carve frozen wood products, but it's usually simpler to carve green wood.

Green wood simply implies that it still has moisture in it, that it has been newly trimmed.

You can chop a piece of wood and freeze it to assist contain moisture and greenness.

Keeping a piece of wood in the refrigerator or leaving it in the snow or outside if it remains below freezing is a nice way to keep the moisture in your green wood until you can get around to building it.

Place green wood in a plastic bag to assist maintain the moisture, even if it is in the refrigerator or freezer (think of the freezer burner).

I placed wood in a flowing stream or pond and held it immersed as weights by stones. This operates in a pinch for a short time, but ultimately it will start to die and discolor if left underwater for more than a couple of days.

If you chop a new tree and then let it lie in the sun, your wood will begin to dry out and often trigger splits or controls to grow.

So if you've discovered some green wood, it's better to go ahead and carve it as quickly as feasible. Otherwise, placed it in the refrigerator or freezer until you get to it.

Wood can be stored in a freezer for years in plastic. I like to re-wet the bottom of the wood before packaging it in plastic to lend it a coating of foam on the ground, I believe it's an additional drying insurance.

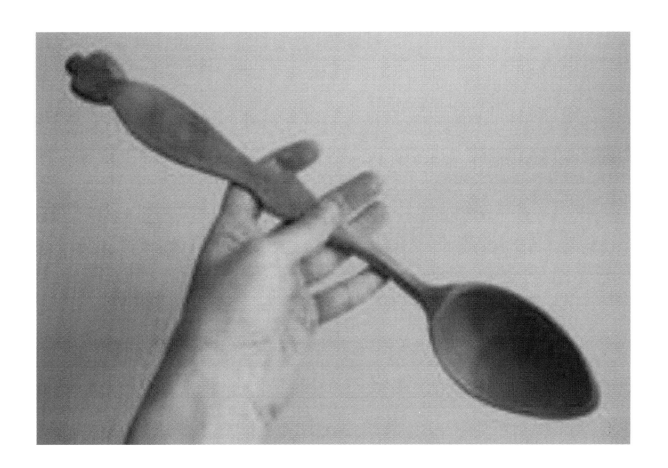

Dimensions: The size of the tree or branch will, of course, dictate the scope of your venture. I'm going to list some overall guidelines Chopsticks only need a branch or shoot about 1/2 "to 3/4" in diameter, about 12 "long.

You need a limb that is not much bigger than about 4 "in diameter for a serving spoon. You can get away with a lower spoon diameter, maybe down to 2 "in diameter. If you're going to do a ladle, you need to discover something with a bigger diameter.

Crookedness and imperfections: Straight grained timber is simple to discover, you can often just get a piece of firewood and divide a piece for a spoon or some other project.
Personally, I believe that more exciting looking spoons are generally produced from bent branches, so keep your eye out for bent wood and seek it out.

You're going to want to maintain an eye out for knots and other imperfections that might render it hard to carve your spoon.
Aim for timber that doesn't have a bunch of knots in it if you've discovered a piece of green wood you want to inspect for the deformities in the bark that would reveal where the concealed leaves have grown. You might find that only the top part of the limb has nodes and hidden branches, while the bottom part doesn't, so you might be prepared to use only half of it.

I'm going to get more data about spoon design, layout and likely something about steam bending timber for bent spoons in a potential blog post. For now, I'm hoping that this will get things going in the correct direction for budding green woodworkers.

BEST KNIFE FOR WHITTLING

Perhaps the most important whittling tool is a knife, because without it, we would only have a bit of un-carved wood. Although they might seem like simple tools, there are a lot of different knives on the market today, some of which are good options for whittling and others that are only used for other purposes. If you're going to get a new knife when you embark on a new whittling hobby, here are some potential options:

Opinel Carbon Steel Folding Everyday Carry Locking Pocket Knife

Simple and durable weapon, this folding pocket knife is a classic choice for whittling and carrying every day. Opinel carbon steel is extremely hard and durable, which means that it cuts well, resists wear and is easy to sharpen. Plus, all of the Opinel knives are made with their signature Virobloc safety ring to fix the knife open while you're whittling.

Pros: Cheap Durable blade that can be quickly sharpened Easy-to-use blade lock
Cons: Carbon steel blade corrodes if wet.

Wood Carving Sloyd Knife

This Sloyd wood carving knife features a short, pointed tip for delicate wood cutting and precise work. The high-quality carbon steel blade allows a good, straight cut through both soft and hardwood, which is great from a whittler's point of view. Plus, the ergonomically designed handle is made of oak and rubbed with linseed oil for easier grip after hours of use.

Morakniv Wood Carving 106 Knife WithLaminated Steel Blade, 3.2-Inch

The Morakniv Wood Carving Knife is a precision whittling knife made in Sweden since 1891. With an ergonomic handle made of oiled birch, this is the kind of knife that feels great in your hand after hours of whittling. The knife also has a 3.2 inch long, robust, laminated steel handle, favored by greenwood workers around the world.

Pros: Super durable laminated steel blade
Convenient oiled birch handle
The fixed blade comes with a sheath

Flexcut Right-Handed Carvin' Jack

If you know that one tool just isn't enough for all your wood carving and whittling needs, Flexcut Right-handed Carvin ' Jack might be a multi-tool for you. This jackknife is made of 6 different carving-specific edges and is built for right-handed whittlers. This contains a chisel, a carving knife, a hook knife, a v-scorp, a gouge scorp, and a straight gouge, which ensures that you can finish every task.

Flexcut JKN88 Whittling' Jack, With 1-1/2 Inch Detail Knife And 2-Inch Roughing Knife

If you want the ability to have several whittling tools but don't want the weight, size, and cost of a large multi-tool, the FlexcutWhittlin ' Jack might be what you're looking for. Designed with two whittling-specific knives, including a 1.5-inch specification knife and a 0.5-inch roughing knife,

STEP BY STEP CARVING TUTORIAL

SPOON CARVING

A few years earlier, my mother smashed a inexpensive wooden spoon in the kitchen. She turned to me and said, "How difficult would it be for you to create a wooden spoon?"I had a few hand tools, and we started experimenting with whatever scraps of wood we had on hand.

Eventually, I discovered that traditional wooden spoons were lap-sculpted from green wood, but I was already well on my manner to creating a technique that operated well in dry difficult woods. Since then, I've produced hundreds of spoons and spatulas in many dimensions, from two-foot-long stirring spoons to two-inch serving spoons. Spoon making is quick, too. Once you learn the methods, you can go from inventory choice to finishing in one hour.

Stock SelectionMany hardwoods are suitable for creating spoons, but the thicker the grain and the less open the pores, the easier. You can exercise white pine, but a hardwood spoon is better suited for harsh use in the kitchen. Choose a hardwood for your first spoon, such as poplar, black walnut, soft maple or cherry. I have effectively used a lot of forest, including pecan, orange Osage, Chinese tallow tree and mesquite. Once you get the feel of it, attempt difficult trees like beech or hard maple. Eventually, you're going to look for a inventory of angles and twists that seem to encourage you to make a spoon.

Choose a straight, transparent piece of timber 1/2" to 3/4" dense, 10" to 12" long and 2" to 3" broad. The spoons in the lead picture (above) all began with a piece of inventory that was 3/4" dense and 12" long. Your spoon size may differ depending on your private preferences. It doesn't matter if the inventory is cropped or twisted, but there must be no end controls to make the tray. I'm going to bet that you already have an suitable item in your off-cut bin.

Many hardwoods are suitable for creating spoons, but the thicker the grain and the less open the pores, the easier. You can exercise white pine, but a hardwood spoon is better suited for harsh use in the kitchen. Choose a hardwood for your first spoon, such as poplar, black walnut, soft maple or cherry. I have effectively used a lot of forest, including pecan, orange Osage, Chinese tallow tree and mesquite. Once you get the feel of it, attempt difficult trees like beech or hard maple. Eventually, you're going to look for a inventory of angles and twists that seem to encourage you to make a spoon.

Choose a straight, transparent piece of timber 1/2" to 3/4" dense, 10" to 12" long and 2" to 3" broad. The spoons in the lead picture (above) all began with a piece of inventory that was 3/4" dense and 12" long. Your spoon size may differ depending on your private preferences. It doesn't matter if the inventory is cropped or twisted, but there must be no end controls to make the tray. I'm going to bet that you already have an suitable item in your off-cut bin.

Design

First, create a cardstock model. Good handles are generally no longer than 3/4" broad and are often smaller. The serving spoon containers are generally about 2" broad and 3" to 4" long, while the mixing spoons are lower, with containers about 11/2" broad and no longer than 3" long. But let your private opinions be your guide. Some individuals like parallel-sided handles, while others like swelling at the bottom and tapering toward the jar. Serving spoons have large, profound bowls, but they often have brief handles. Mixing spoons requires small bowls and stiff handles.

An easy way to create a model is to draw a centerline on a sheet of paper, draw half the picture of your spoon on one part of the board, wrap the paper on the board, and trim your profile. Unfold your document, and you have a completely symmetrical model. After I produced a few dozen spoons and realized what forms I enjoyed best, I produced several wooden templates to speed up this job.

Plane down one side of the wood to render the design lines easier to see. Draw your spoon layout onto your inventory, ensuring that the grain goes directly through the full spoon. It can assist draw the center line down the spoon pot. Sketch out the inside of the freehand jar, leaving a 1/16" cap.

Begin By Dishing The Bowl

It's best to form the inside of the jar first, then the knob, and lastly the outside of the box. That manner, you'll always have parallel surfaces to safely clamp in the target as you form the spoon. Secure your inventory and keep your gouge in both palms.

The strong gouge is going to slice well, both with the grain and across it. Make your roughing cuts across the grain and the end cuts of the grain. Place the gouge on one side of the table close the centerline to grind out the box. As you press the edge into the wood, shift the grip sideways, creating a cut. Repeat, using overlapping strokes, until you reach the other end of the tub. Turn the inventory around and operate the other hand of the target. Gradually, operate home on your design lines. Now bring the light slices of the grain, starting at the front of the jar. The jar should gradually move from the front to the back. Get the ground as clean as you can with your gouge.

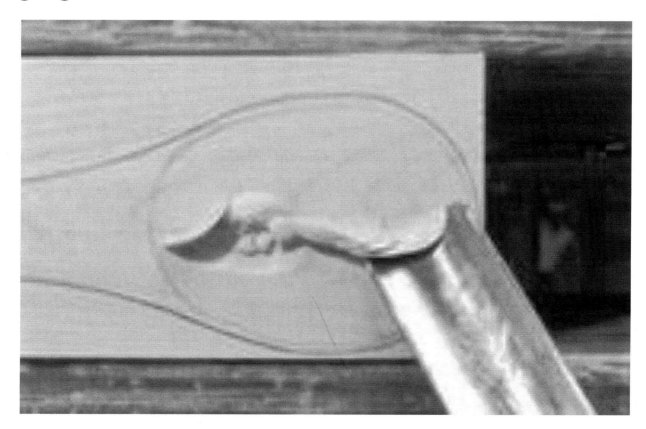

Push the gouge into the wood, running right across the grain. Then shift the tool to create a cutting slice laterally. It's best to remove the wood from the middle of the tray first.

Use overlapping reductions to gradually get back to the design lines. Use softer cuts, with the grain, to deepen the jar. Remove the bucket as well as you can with the gouge.

Shape The Handle

The most convenient handle form is either straight and broad or half-round in cross-section, with a straight handle at the bottom of the frame. Use your preferred technique of slicing bends to smooth out the handle and the outer profile of the jar. I use a drawknife, but the group saw is going to operate, too. If you choose to use a drawknife, note: when producing a plain or concave surface, use it with a bevel. Use the bevel up when forming a convex surface.

When the majority of the waste is taken, use a spokeshave to form the grip. Depending on the path of the grain, you may need to press or grab the spokeshave. Start with the sides of the handle, work down to the design lines. Use a scooping movement on the arms when operating the concave walls with a spokeshave, pushing the spokeshave slightly backwards on each stroke. Next, chamfer the bottom of the stick. Then release each of the six angles, sweeping the bottom of the handle as uniformly as necessary.

It is feasible to create the handle too small and sensitive at this stage, but starting spoon carvers are more probable to err on the fat hand. Shape the handle to make it convenient in your hand— the design lines are a visual guide, but trust your fingers as well. As the grip thins, you'll feel it flexing beneath your instruments, and you may think that you're trying to drop it. Don't care about it. If the spoon survives the method of its own creation, it will stay in the kitchen for many years to come.

You don't have to round the bottom of the strap, but it feels good. If you have to, you can drill a hole for sticking in the end, but most individuals maintain their spoons in bags or canisters.

Cut out the bowl profile and manage it. Hand saws and electric saws are both working well. Then use a spokeshave to bend the curves down to the design rows. The spokeshave excels in shaping the handle. To create a half-round cross-section, chamfer the edges and extract the angles.Shape The Outside Of The Bowl

Now transform the spoon around in the jar and operate on the outside of the jar. Use a drawknife or a handsaw to form three big chamfers, two on each hand and one at the bottom. Use a spokeshave to round the corners of the facets. Start each slice on one hand of the tray and follow the top of the inventory to the middle of the jar. Move to the reverse hand after a few taps on one hand. Quick, light strokes are the best work.

Remove the bulk of the inventory from the floor of your spoon's bucket by removing big facets. You're going to refine the form as you go.

As you form the outside of the jar, stop frequently to measure the size of the jar by pinching it between your fingers. It's optimal between 3/16" and 1/8" dense. Theoretically, the outside of the jar should be the same shape as the inside, and should be the same density from the tip to the knees. In reality, the density may differ slightly from front to back. Just make sure you don't leave too much wood on the bottom of the tray, particularly close the top. The top of the spoon should bend softly so that the bottom of the cabinet or the inside of the mixing bowl can be readily scraped.

Use the spokeshave to narrow down the shoulders. Use the same scooping movement that you used on the sides. Purpose to remove wood from the arms without proceeding to thin down the grip. It's simple to leave too much wood here, creating a heavy, bulky spoon in use. Half-round.

rasp is a nice solution to talking rasp.

Ease sharp corners with the spokeshave. Control your cut by holding it one-handed, thumb on the workpiece.

Don't leave too much wood where the handle joins the tray. You don't want to make your spoon thick and bulky when it's in use.

As you work, periodically take the workpiece out of the lens and look at it from a variety of angles from the top, from the side, and down the length to make sure you don't have lumps or spots remaining anywhere. The bottom of the container should bend down below the grip row, and the handle should be either directly or mildly bent downwards.

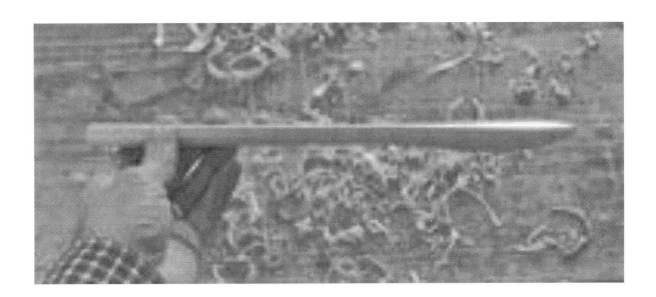

The bottom of the jar should fall significantly below the bottom of the handle. The bottom of the spoon may be directly or mildly bent.

Finishing

Once the spoon has a suitable shape, use card scrapers to remove tool marks and tears. I use a bent card scraper inside the cabinet. I use a slim, straight card scraper, hooked between my palms, for everything else. Use lengthy, soft strokes to mix the lines together and extract the remains of your design lines. The only smooth floor should be on the bottom of the grip, where the thumb rests in use. Apply a non-toxic oil finish after sanding to 220-grit.

Smoothing Out The Bowl.

Use card scrapers to extract tool marks and tears. A bent card scraper allows a brief effort to smooth out the tray.

Sand your spoon to 220-grit, then add non-toxic petroleum (e.g. butcher block, pumpkin, chicken or chicken oil).

Wooden spoons should be cleaned by side with periodic soap and water.

Don't let them soak in water for a long time, and never bring them in the dishwasher, which will lead the wood to deteriorate rapidly. A nice spoon is supposed to last in the kitchen for many years, but it will eventually wear out. If splits grow in the pot, it's time to remove your spoon. It's time to create another one.

CARVING A WOODEN GNOME FROM SALVAGED WOOD

How to create a wooden figurine of a gnome. It's really a easy job, and let's get began for the most portion.

Step 1: Wood Salvage Wood Selection is essential when you start whittling. Many gave up, having picked up a piece of wood that was unworkable, a malleable wood sort important to a nice first-time experience. I completed a DIY project in the 9th grade on whittling for my English honors class, but I failed terribly and ended up demonstrating my class how to bring together a skateboard. It was a horrible chasm.

So, this is a scheme of 15 years in movement. It's always been on the back of my mind, so when I was jogging one weekend, I saw splintered wood dividers from various car accidents, and I asked it's soft wood. I picked up a piece and brought it back home.

As I looked at it, I discovered some termites, so I was treating the wood with some termite spray that I was lucky enough to have. I let it go for a day, and then I cleaned it with soap. It was prepared to go.

(There are some good pieces that I'm thinking of saving and turning into totem poles.) You don't want to spend time squeezing your fingers with a stick, so get your jigsaw out and bring your wood in your target-grip and chop it down. After the first cut, the pencil is in a rough form. The image below is truly a digital instance, because I began this project before I thought about sharing it.

Step 3: Xacto Knife Callousing So, the finest blade to begin is simply a long blade, which I think is the ideal whittling tool. It only makes sense with lengthy strokes.

Continue drawing your forms and features until you finally get something like this.

Step 4: Paint Your Wood I used acrylic foundation materials and blended with the required colours. Actually, I did a pair of distinct parts of paint and altered the colors until I enjoyed the image.

Anyway, this is simple things, but maybe it's going to encourage somebody.

Carving Jack-O-Lanterns From Scrap Wood

I wanted something enjoyable to do with my children for my second Maker in Residence venture. They can be produced with wood scraps from other initiatives, and they can be completed with what you have on hand. The only stuff I purchased for this venture was a saw-tooth hanger on the back of the Jack-O-Lanterns. (Only because I was too poor to create it). Let's get to operate now!

Step 1: Choose Your Material and Mark Out Your Pattern

I stared at the edges of the store and discovered these two cuts. One was 10 "wide, and two" dense, tough, blue pine. The other panel was 12"x20 "and 3/4 dense poplar, which had been mounted. The children and I used to draw our designs on the panels and they were nice enough to show for me!

Step 2: Cut Out Your Pattern

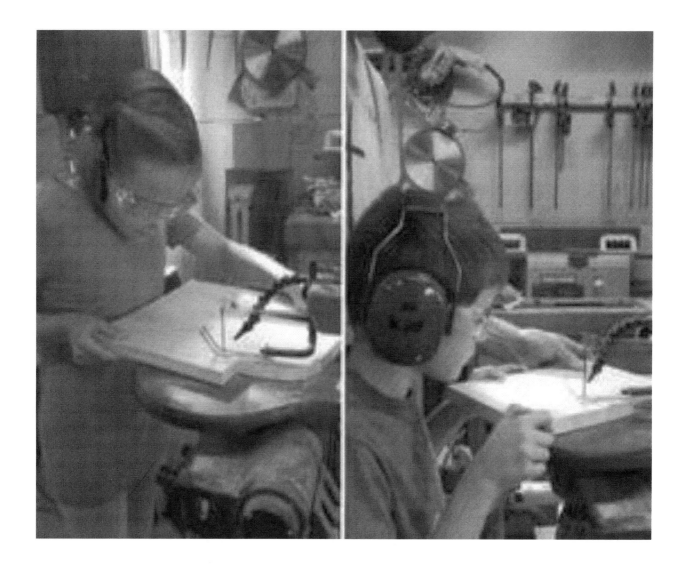

Next, we went to see the scroll. This was before I got my Dremel Moto-Saw, so we used my normal scroll saw instead. I've been scrolling with my sister for 8 or 9 months now, so she's fairly great at it. I was a little concerned about my seven-year-old kid, but he did a excellent job! As a matter of reality, all he wishes to do now is break stuff off, and he's really great at it!

It's fairly easy to follow the blade row, you could use a group saw or a jig saw, or even a coping saw to do this portion. Don't worry about the tools you don't have (YET) but find out how to do the initiatives with what you do!

Step 3: Add a Cleat, and Start Carving

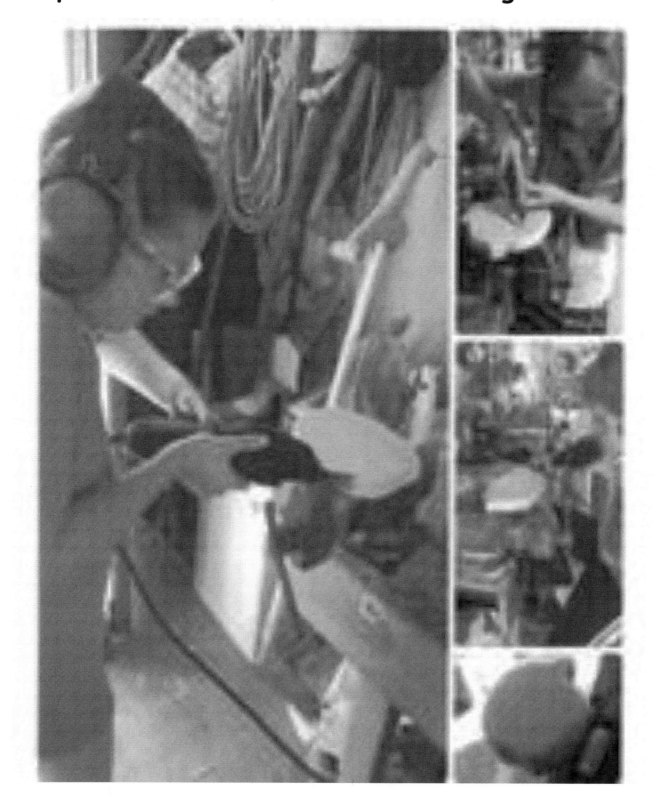

Now that we've got the wood cut to form, we need to keep it constant to operate on it. I sliced some 1 "scrap material into 4" sections, drilled two holes in each and attached it to the back of each project. We could now clamp down on our job in a vice and have both palms to regulate our instruments. We began carving by breaking down the corners of our designs with a Dremel Multi Max oscillating instrument with a tight wood cutting blade inside. The simplest way to do this is to keep the blade at an angle to the sharp edge and break the sheets off, varying corners to remove distinct quantities of content. When we formed the corners, We twisted the Multi-Max until the blade was on its rim and carved into the faces, faces and mouths, this is an easy way to smooth the Jack-O-Lanterns characteristics. When the rough sculpture was completed, we switched to our Dremel 7700 with a conical slicing tool to wash the corners and add information. As with all instruments, make sure you brace yourself when using a rotary tool, so you have more power over the part.

Step 4: Sanding!!!

Okay, nobody enjoys sand, but it makes a enormous distinction to the completed item. We installed a sanding board on the Multi-Max and began with 60 grit, working our way through 220. I like sanding with this instrument because I can get it to narrow places and change the power level. You could use a random orbital sander, a palm sander... whatever you've got, the job will be done, including records and side sanding.

Step 5: Finish Work

This is always a pleasant component of it! You can use whatever you have around the room to do this, like spray paint, finger paint, water branding, etc.

That said, we chose to use Fiber reactive dye, because I've already had some of the last moment we tie-dyed shirts. We rubbed the orange dye on the Jack-O-Lanterns, washed our hands, and used the green dye for the flowers. This is when one manufacturer deviated from the course, while Tennessee and I used a sharpie to add information to our sculptures, Jay was busy gluing scraps of wood into bottle caps, which he then attached to his eye pumpkin! When we were pleased with our designs, I brought them outside and brushed them with Helmsman's wood sealer. After all this fun in the store, I was exhausted, so instead of creating brackets, I purchased them. You can, at most hardware stores, too!

Step 6: Step Back, and Admire!

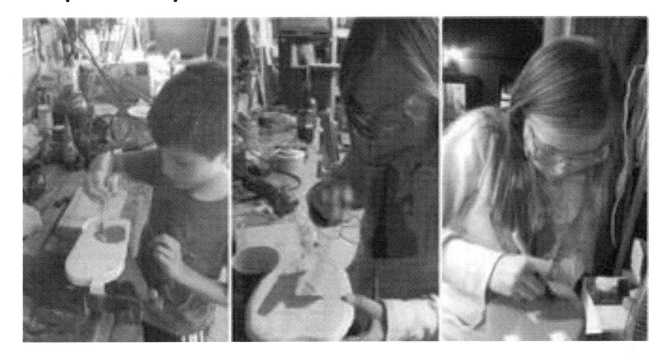

Here are the initiatives that have been completed. I picked them up with pride! Everyone says that Jay's Jack-O-Lantern is the coolest, even though Tenn's is fairly darn adorable, too! Now, bring some kind of exercise.

HAND CARVED PIZZA WHEEL

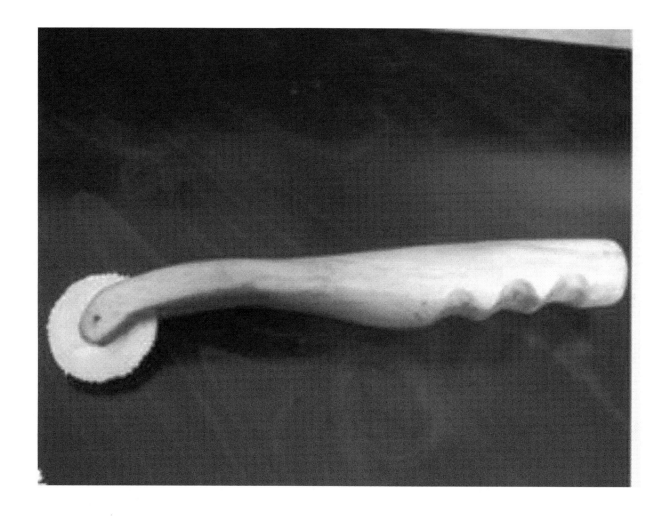

Don't you hate it when you cook Pizza in your home and you can't split Pizza in equal portions... well, that's what occurred to me and I chose to create my private Pizza accessories.

Step 1: Stuff. Materiales.

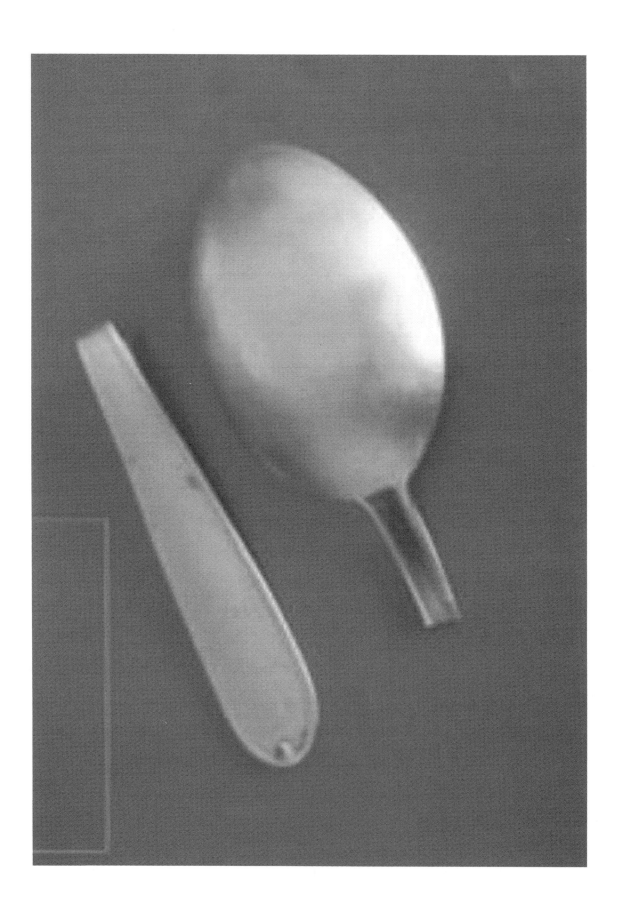

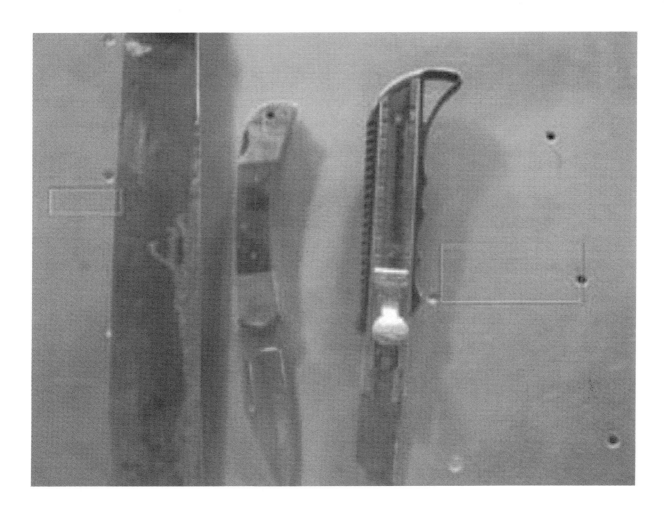

- Stainless Spoon.
- Piece of Wood.
- Screw.

  Drill.
- Punzon.

  Mask Tape.
- Math Compasses.
- Hammer.

- Machete.

  Buck Knife.

  Cutter.

  Sand .

- Paper.

- Beeswax.

- Varnish. Barniz.

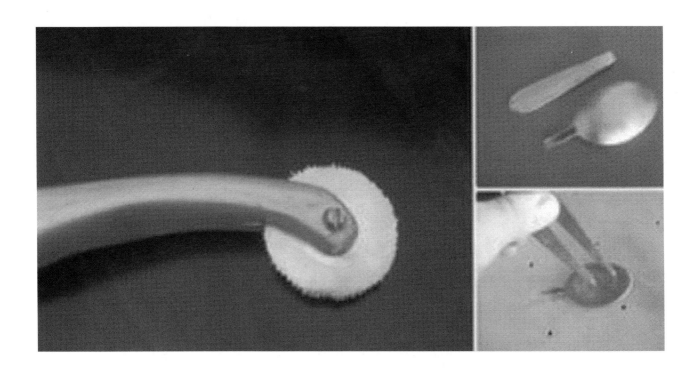

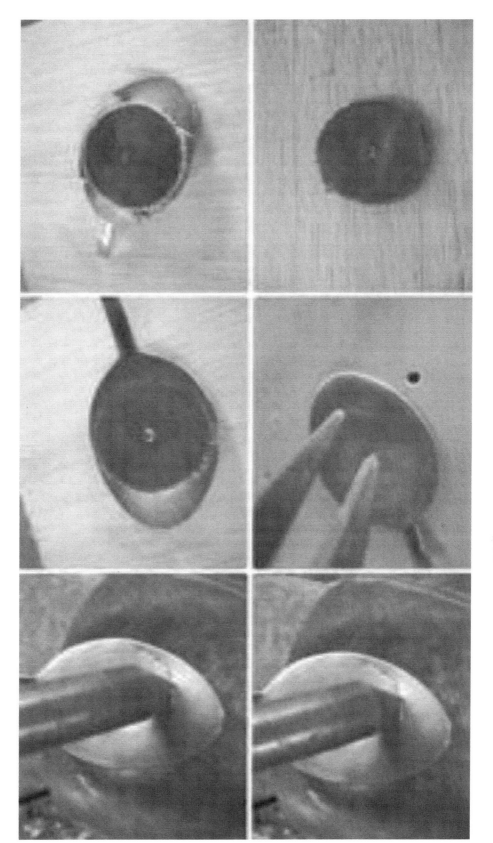

Smash the Spoon over the Anvil, but first cover the Spoon with Leather or Rubber if Hammer doesn't damage the Spoon Surface.

With the assistance of the math compasses, discover the middle of the spoon to draw a circle and dig a 5/32 bracket, then hit the whole box with the steel puncher, with the pliers you had to remove the remaining parts of the Spoon.

File the wheel in the back of the triangle insert.

Step 3: The Handle

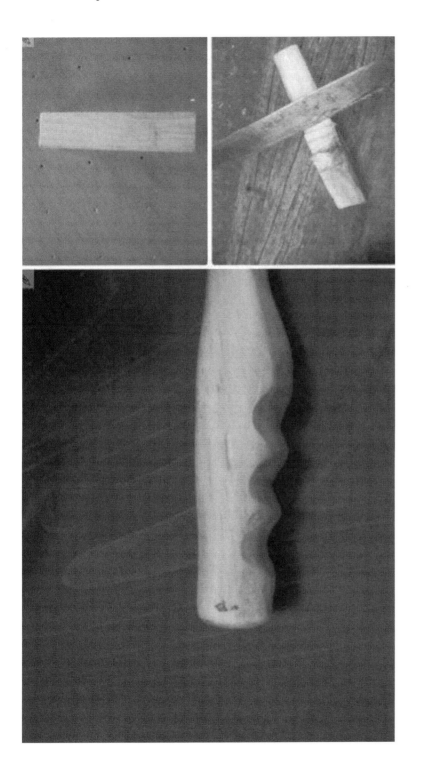

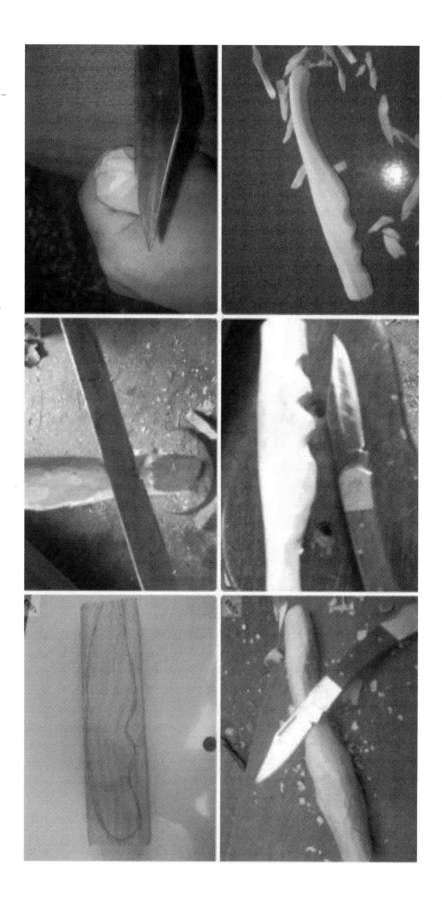

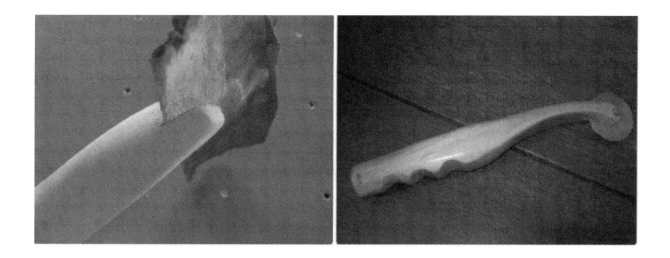

I find a lovely piece of wood, sketch the structure and begin carving with Machete. I handed the form to the texture of the wood.

To brush the corners I took "Mikaela" my favorite trusty buck knife and create ergonomically shaped, sand with distinct kinds of sandpaper, if you want you can engrave whatever you want or carve your name letters; beeswax or varnish it; fix the wheel and that's all. Ready to make a pizza slice.

Step 4: Right On.

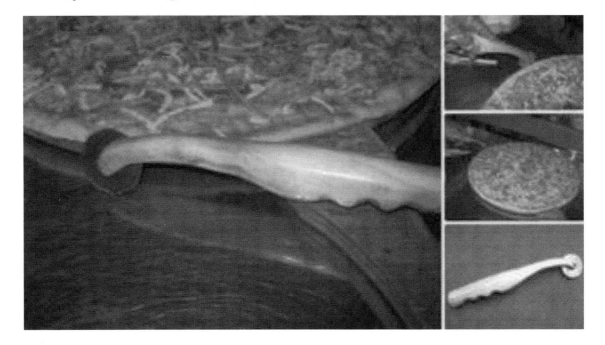

CARVING A EAGLE FEATHER

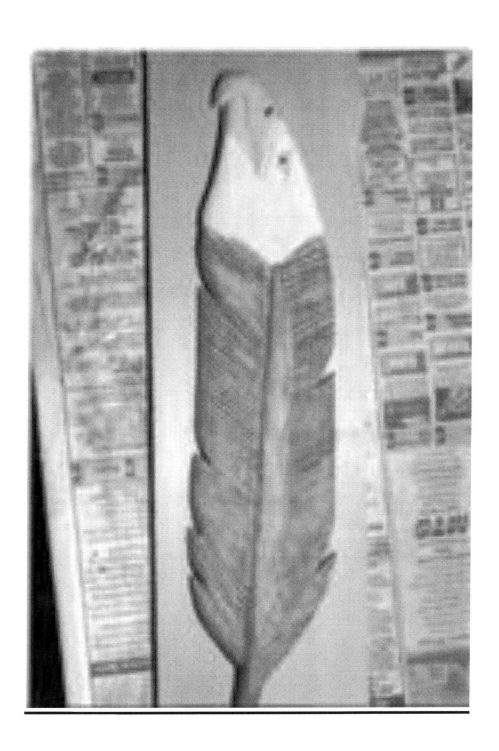

I'm going to demonstrate how to carve a feather with an eagle's head on it. It's a easy carving that a beginner should be prepared to do readily.

Step 1: Items Needed

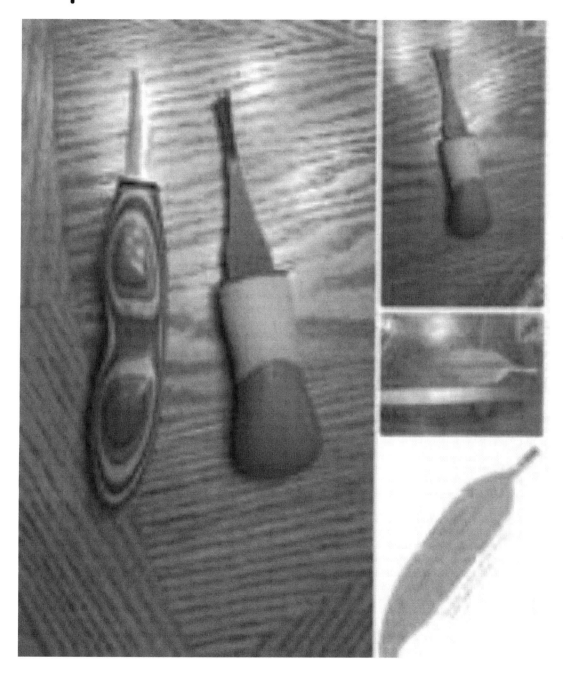

1. The piece of wood is about 14x3x3/8. I used a pallet slat, but any soft wood is going to be okay.

2. It's pattern. I have included one for you to use.

3. Bandsaw or coping has seen

4. A knife, a V-tool, and a gouge would be useful.

5. It's sandpaper.

6. The paintings and the brushes.

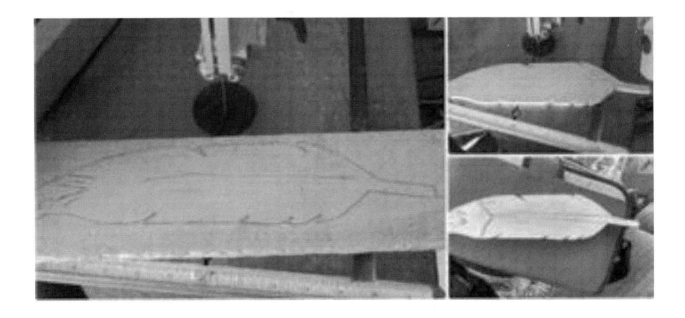

Sand the wood relatively smoothly and trace the model to the wood, then pull it out. I used the group I saw to do this. The band saw saves time, but you can always use the coping saw to do this.

Then draw lines with a pencil in the remainder of the structure.

Step 3: Thin And Round Off Feather

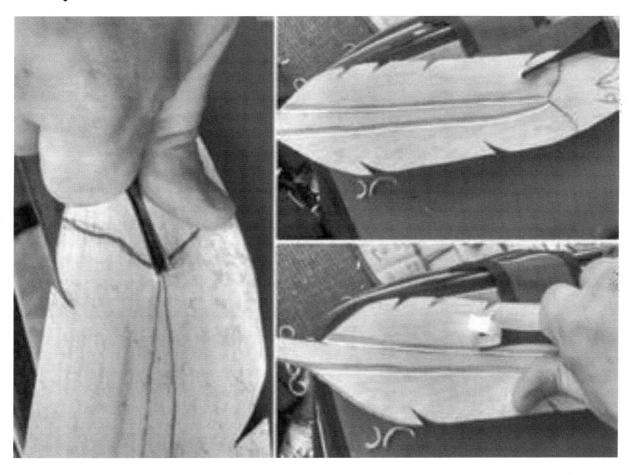

Before you start, always be careful and never cut to any body portion, including your fingers, it's a good idea to use a carving gloves. Plus, always break the grain of the wood, if you break it and the wood begins to tear, you're moving in the wrong direction and need to push it off the other manner. Use the V-tool to create a stop slice along a quill on both ends, so you want to go deep enough to create quill stick out. I'm going to take a few runs to get to the place you want. Don't attempt and do all of this with a single pass, as it's difficult to regulate when you push down tough and dangerous. Take a knife or gouge after the stop break and remove surplus wood from the feather on both ends of the quill. Next, you'll want to round off the feather from the quill to the bottom of the feather.

Step 4: Shape and Round Head

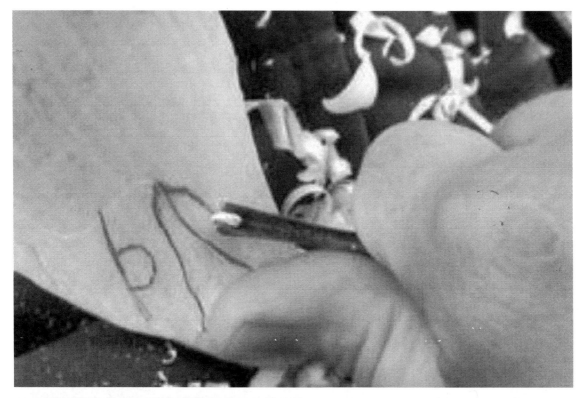

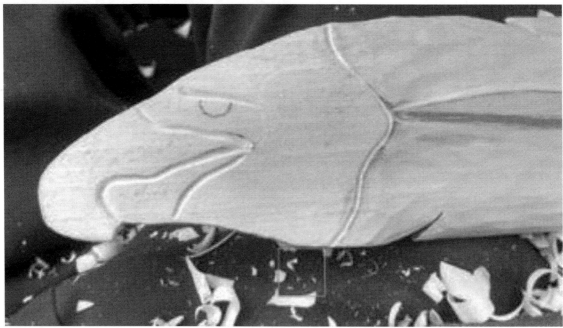

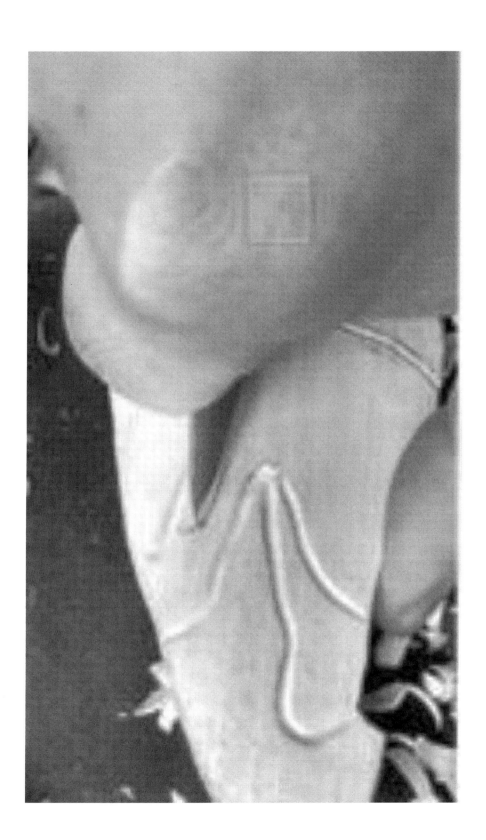

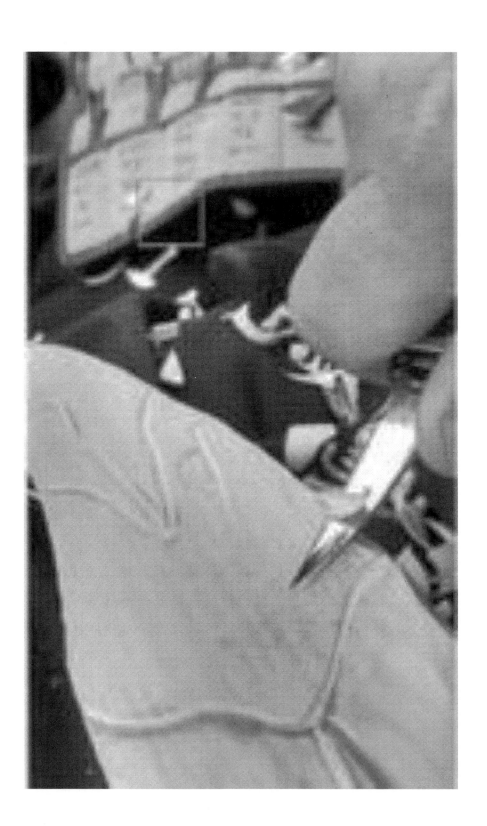

Use the V-tool to create a halt on the beak, the back of the head, and the row above the eye. I like to bring my knife and trim the round shape of the eye, and then squeeze the wood around the ring of the eye to make it stand out a little. Now, turn off the eye. Start to round the corners of the cap and beak. Then chop the beak to the stop cuts. You're going to remove the wood from the beak, so it's lower down than the head. The reduced beak must be closer than the upper beak. Round off all the tough corners of the beak and the top of the eye. I also create sure that there are no saw marks anywhere on the sculpture. Use a knife or a gouge to extract it.

Step 5: Smooth Feather Up

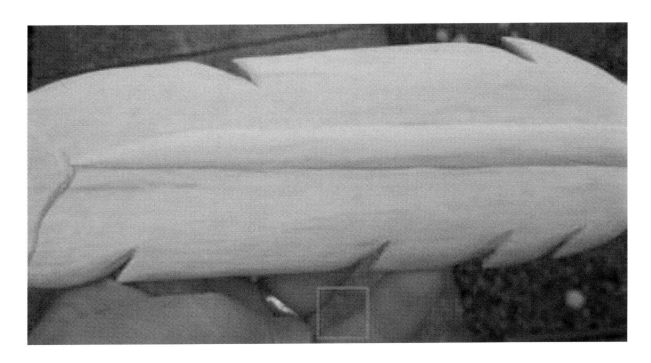

Make sure that the feather is beautifully shaped, then bring the knife and round off the quill and placed a nice taper on the bottom of it, I like sanding the feather a little to smooth it a little, particularly the quill itself. The rest of the feather isn't as essential as that, but I still struck it a little. The top I'm not sanding, but it's up to you.

Step 6: Adding Alot of Lines

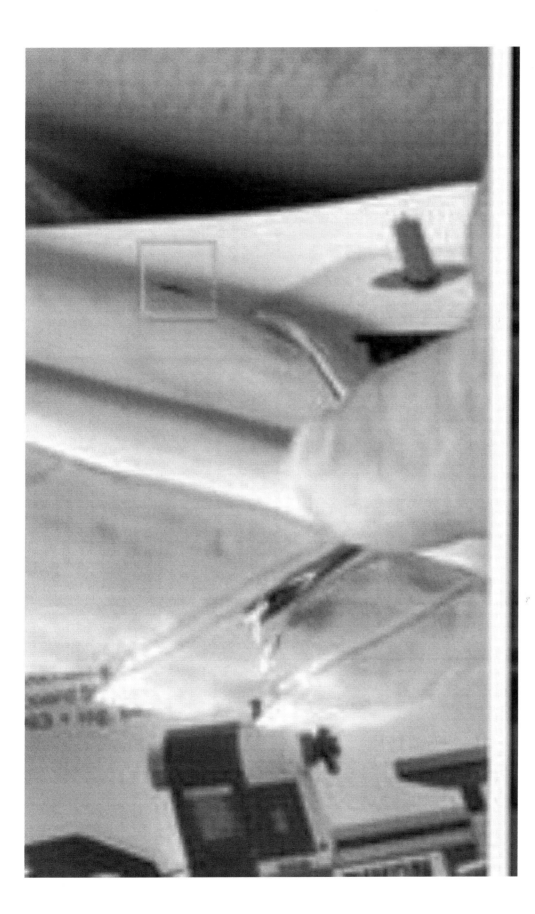

I like to bring my v-tool and slice the first rows out of the ruffles in the feather, so the corners are pretty much the same. Then begin going on with the remainder of the rows.

Step 7: Painting

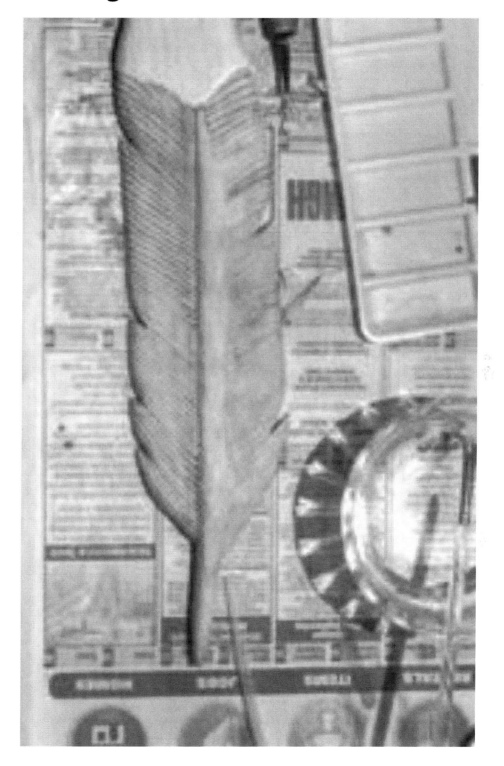

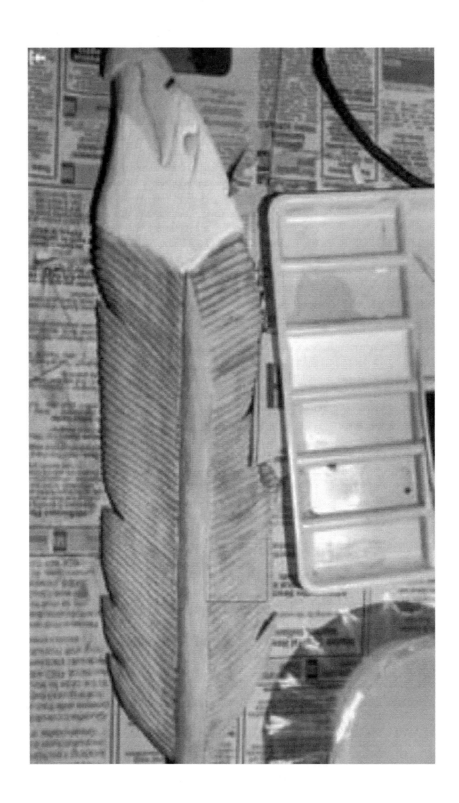

I'm using acrylic paint. The brown one I had a bunch of water down there. It was very runny because I didn't want it to be dark gray. I dilute the white, but not as much as the brown. The blue one was even less, maybe 50/50 with water. The black I used undiluted, and I just took a toothpick to insert a place on it.

CARVED TIKI IDOL

After getting a nice new set of chisels, I thought I was going to try them out. What could I really do on a cold winter night? Something to warm up. Of course, Woody, but with a hint of danger...

Step 1

First, I started doing some work on what Tiki Idols actually look like. To Google, guy! (Other

Internet search engines are available, but a little waste of time). It quickly led me to this interesting wikipedia article on the history of tiki.

Turns out that the whole kitsch shebang is a 20th century American pastiche of Polynesian art. High on rum cocktails with random bits of fruit and hawaiian tops. Two of my favorite stuff!

I began with a 45 mm X 90 mm piece (essentially 2×4 style) of wood construction. This wood is nice and soft, so it's good to start carving. I used a little bit of reclaimed wood from the demolished

I was about to sketch a model. It's pretty basic, but I didn't want to over-design because I knew the result was going to change as part of the carving process.

(At this point, 32 plays later, I started getting a little tired of the song.)

Step 2

The image above illustrates the early stages of the rugged sculpture. This stage only extracts all the excess wood easily before you continue with the info. The eyes and eyebrows wanted a strong straight line, so I used a saw to slice to the gritty length that I wanted. Instead I started cutting around the sides of my lines by pressing the lines with the chisel and the mallet to cleanly slice the grain before the chisel.

Carving is much easier, so you manage to get a lot fewer bruises by using a bench hook. This just sits on the edge of your work table and prevents the wood from slipping away when you chisel.

From this point on, the sculpture was pretty straightforward. Take off small amounts any time you can't cover the log!

The photographs for this stage demonstrate the progress of the carve. When you look closely, you can see the slice rates when I formed the wood.

I find that for decorative carving like this, using your hands to push the chisel through the wood is much more accurate and neat than hammering it through. Soft wood, like the wood I used here, obviously helps, but as long as the chisels are sharp, you can shave the carving material very neatly.

You're going to take really small amounts off at a time, and persistence is key when you build trust and expertise with the chisels.

To offer a better sense of depth, you can slice a little behind the different features of the neck.

I wasn't sure how I wanted to get a nose, but after a little testing, I decided to switch from a plain triangular nose to something much more nostrillous. The design of the eye also changed, and I used a saw to cut some iris-like slits. Projects and proposals still evolve as time passes by!

I cut up the back of the block a bit to give it a more sculpted-from-real-tree look. The finer carved pieces were left thinly cut to give it more of a stone-age look, while the excellent detail was finely crafted. A nice sharp chisel can leave a very smooth surface and is much smoother than sandpaper! Most of the original paint has been stripped like this. It gives a better finish for less effort and time than sanding.

Hold the chisels clean! It's safer and the whole process takes less time and produces better results.

Step 4: Sanding Down

After the carving was more or less finished, I sanded the detail down with 180-grit sandpaper and then gave it a good time with some 240-grit. This makes it feel smooth without feeling too polished.

I like to rub my hands over the wood in order to find any visible rough / pointy bits so that I can smooth them out. And, because I'm a pervert.

While the design was sanded, the majority of the wood was left raw, with just a test on the splinters, to maintain a rugged, desert island appearance like an altar.

While the surface was sanded, the majority of the wood remained raw, with only a test on the splinters.

Then I used a Colron Wood dye to color the light pine in a darker color. I used a combination of 2 parts Red Mahogany to 1 part Indian Rosewood, because the red is too red, but the Indian Rosewood is very, very black!

The ink was rubbed on after the bee had been washed by rubbing all over it with a white spirit filter. It eliminates any sawdust or oil that would prevent the pigment from being ingested properly. Using a comb instead of a roller to add a wood dye makes it easier to carefully dye all the nooks and crannies of the carving, so you don't suddenly notice a patch of undyedplae wood for a couple of weeks.

After dyeing, I went all over the wood with some 180-grit sandpaper. It brings out the grain in the wood, as the thick portion of the grain does not retain as much of the dye as the rest of the wood, and a small bit of sanding makes the grain stand out, giving a lovely woody appearance!

No lacquer was used to maintain a more natural wood effect.

NATURAL ELBOW BOOMERANG

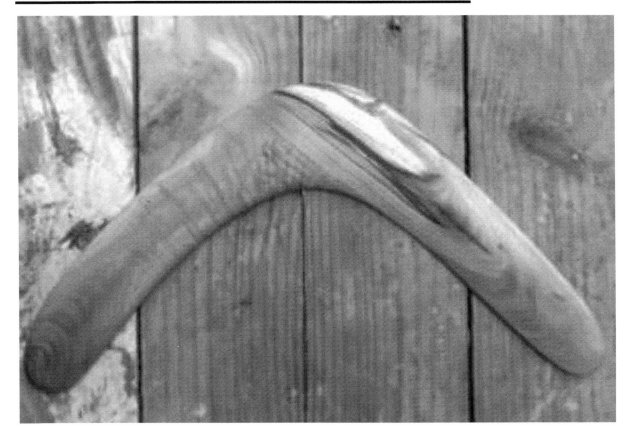

I've been designing, producing and throwing boomerangs for many years. At the start, my booms are made of plywood, a cheap and easy-to-use material—all you need is some plywood, a jigsaw and some sanding paper. Boys are growing up, and people always want more. So I wanted to make my projects a little more exciting and to discover a whole new world: natural boomerangs, or better' natural elbow boomerangs!'

Natural elbow boomerangs are made from elbows that can be seen on almost any tree (you can also find natural' Y's'). Actually living in the suburbs of Southern France, I work with the local species: Holm oak (Quercus ilex) and Olive (Oleaeuropaea). In this Instructable, I'm going to show you how to make a boomerang made of olive. You'll see, making this kind of boomerang is really fun, and once you get going, you'll never see plywood again.

All you need:
pocket saw
grafting wax
polyurethane glue
manual saw
vice

plane (electric is highly recommended)

jigsaw

sander

sanding paper (from 80 to 600)

safety gloves, goggles & ear plugs

natural oil

Step 1: Find A Natural Elbow

First approach:' I'm going out for a drive and I'm trying to see what I'm going to find.' Not poor at all, go sniffing in the woods, and I'm sure you're going to find it.

Second approach: choose your species of wood, find the right trees and test the elbows. If you're hunting for Sequoia-stuff you're going to need a telescope and some climbing equipment. The benefit of Olive is that it is a small species with a lot of potential booms that can be easily reached from the surface.

If you have a chance to find a dead tree, you can miss the next move.

Search for trees with a diameter of more or less than 10 cm (3 inches). The more rounded, the stronger. Split the branch with your pocket saw, split the elbow off the tree, and cover the wastewood, and take it all with you. Don't forget to put some grafting wax on your left cut.

A year later, I discovered this in an ancient and neglected orchard in Southern France.

Step 2: Let It Dry

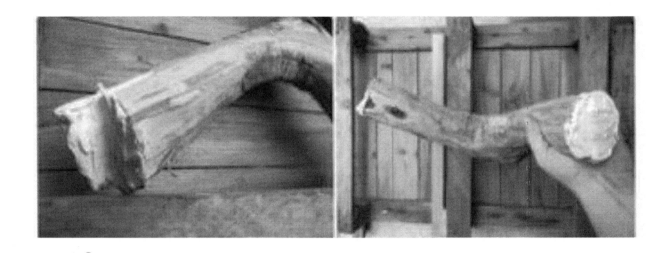

New wood is not ideal for direct handling. Of course, you've got to dry it. I typically cut off the bark with a knife to fasten this process and seal both ends of the elbow with polyurethane-glue. You can use candle wax as well. This prevents the wood from drying and cracking too quickly. Give it some space one year is goodand put it in a well-ventilated location. Do not put it in direct sunlight or on a radiator. The faster it will cool, the better.

Note: the pictures show two different elbows. One of them sliced, one not.

Step 3: Preparing The Elbow

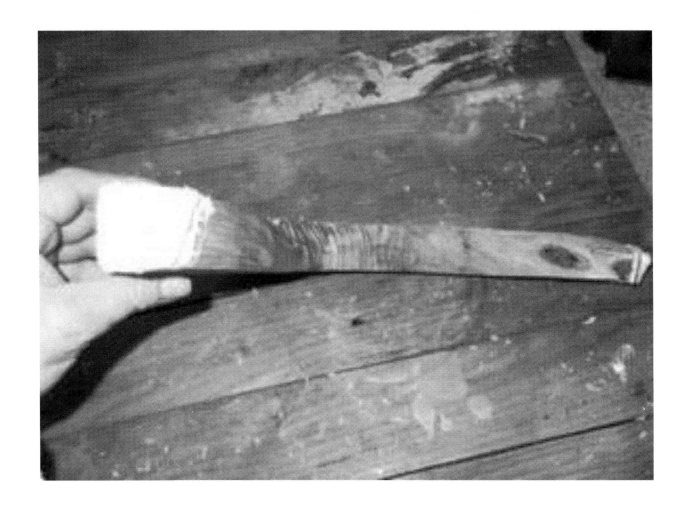

After all, our elbow is clean and we're good to go. It doesn't look very good yet, but three boomerangs are concealed inside this piece of wood. Before we go to slice the elbow into bits that we have to clean, which means we're going to design it to have a flat surface on both sides with a thickness that's almost the same everywhere.

Use an electric plane and don't forget to wear safety gloves, glasses and earplugs.

Step 4: Slicing

The larger the size of the elbow, the more slices you can make. I usually try to see 1 cm (1/3 inch) thick boards. Lock the elbow in the snap and cut it with a manual saw. I'm not suggesting electric saws. Circular saws are too difficult to handle, too dangerous, and I don't have great jigsaw souvenirs. A good old, well-cutting saw is going to do the job very well. You'll be engulfed in the scent of wood in this process. Each plant has its own scent, but I'm sure there's nothing better than the smell of freshly cut olive-wood: a combination of grapes and cherries!

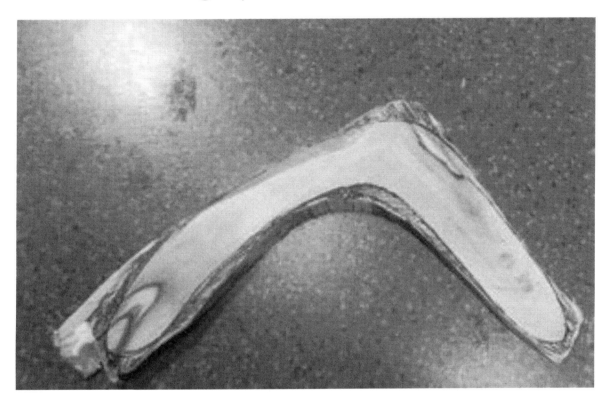

You have at least one piece of your elbow now, time for real work. You don't have to think a lot about it, the tree did this job for you. Look carefully at the structure of the wood and take advantage of the opportunities it offers you. Let the creativity go, draw a few clear lines and get back to work. Don't forget: the tree shaped your boomerang, all you're doing is fine-tuning your work.

In this step, you use a sander, a jigsaw and a helicopter. You can use a sander (I put mine in a vice) to cut small sections. You can use the jigsaw for the remainder. You can always alter the shape of your boom during this stage (first I tried to make an asymmetrical boomerang, then I changed my mind and opted for a more typical shape).

Optional: When this form is finished, you should pay attention to the thickness (I usually make my boomerangs thinner in the middle). Use a flight to do this.

Step 7: Profiling - Basic Boomerang Aerodynamics

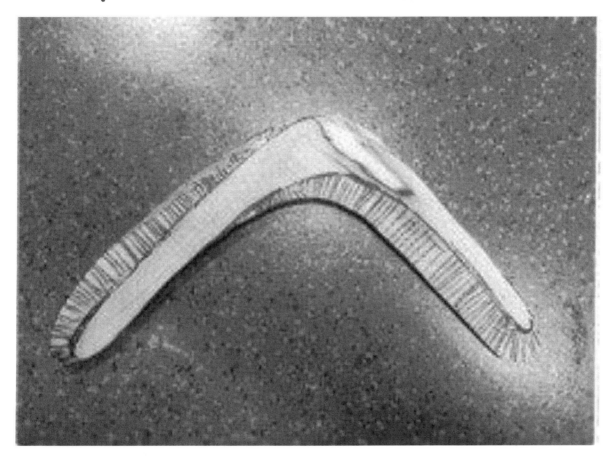

A boomerang is a set of wings that are put together in a certain way. Wings are profiled and rounded at their ends. You need to learn certain basic principles to understand why and how boomerangs work.

Boomerangs are not just going away and coming back. The main reason they're doing this is that they're turning around their axe very quickly after they've been thrown. You're giving it the required spin when tossing a boomerang the right way. This action is counterclockwise (for a right-handed boomerang), leading edges (steep wing-sides) slicing the wind, just like ships, birds, etc. The rotation allows them uplift, and the positioning of the wings causes them to spin. The spin causes the rocket not just to float right away. Translated: the rocket is coming home. Keep these basics in mind while setting up a profile or download a picture. This drawing-thing is not the exact science, sanding and feeling will do the rest of it.

Forming the profiles is sanding, sanding and, in general, sanding: hard (electric) sanding with rough grain at the start and manual sanding with finer grains to finish. This phase is pure instinctive, so try to make the best wing profiles you can get. And take the time.

Note: I never throw away sawdust or wood chips because they're the perfect thing to smoke trout.

Step 8: Oiling

Your boomerang is almost over. All you've got to do is give it some security. Some prefer lacquer, others epoxy, I prefer natural oil. Nothing is more exciting than putting oil on your hands, heating it up and giving the freshly made boomerang its first massage. Clean the excess oil with a piece of cloth and give it a second wash the next day.

Step 9: Throwing!

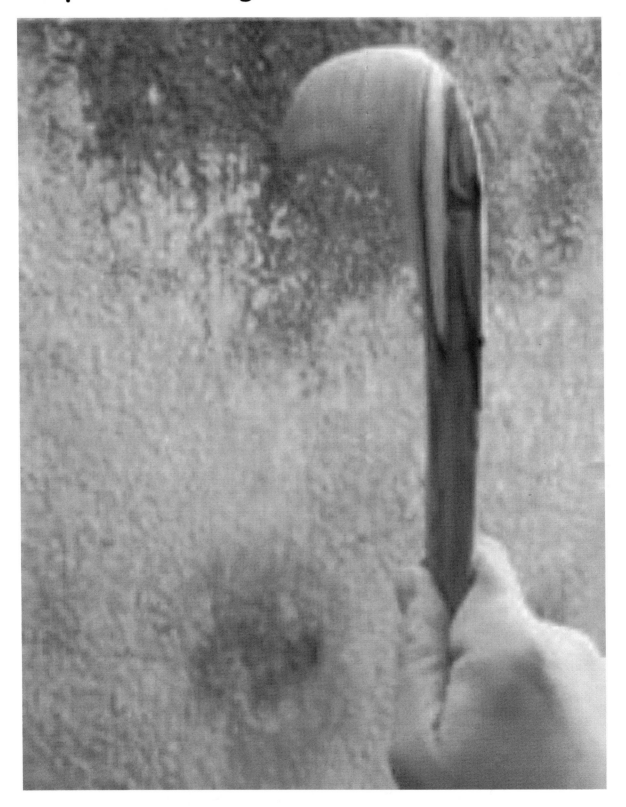

CONCLUSION

Whittling is a form of art, and like all art, you need to find a technique or style that works best for you. Each piece of wood and every knife will feel different in your hands, and what you do with these things will be unique.

my advice, huh? Let's start slowly and easily. Choose a smooth wood that is easy to cut and a knife that feels comfortable in your hands. Get a pair of gloves or a thumb guard for some extra security while learning the different cuts and being conservative in your movements. Over time, you build the confidence you need to try out new techniques and make more elaborate designs.

The design of the wood being carved restricts the size of the carver in that the wood is not equally strong in all directions: it is an anisotropic material. The direction in which the wood is best is referred to as "grain" (grain may be flat, interlocked, wavy or fiddleback, etc.). It's wise to place the more delicate parts of the model along the grain instead of across it. Sometimes, however, the "axis of best fit" is used instead, since the model may have several weak points in different directions, or the position of those points along the grain may entail a precise shaping of the final grain (which is considerably more difficult). Carving blanks are also sometimes assembled, as with carousel horses, out of many smaller boards, and in this way it is possible to orient different areas of carving in the most logical way, both for the carving process and for the durability. More generally, this same method is applied to stronger pieces of wood, where the fork between two branches is used for its divergent grain, or the branch off of a wider log is cut into a beak (this was the technique used for typical Welsh shepherd's crooks and some Native American adze handles). Lack to understand these primary rules can be seen on a continuous basis in damaged construction, when it is observed that while tendrils, tips of birds beaks, etc., arranged across the grain have been split, similar features, built more in accordance with the growth of the wood and not too deeply undercut, remain intact.

Kind reader,

Thank you very much, I hope you enjoyed the book.

Can I ask you a big favor?

I would be grateful if you would please take a few minutes to leave me a gold star on Amazon.

Thank you again for your support.

Antony McDeere

Made in the USA
San Bernardino, CA
24 July 2020